FROM APPLE SEED TO APPLESAUCE

FROM APPLE SEED TO APPLESAUCE

Hannah Lyons Johnson
photographs by Daniel Dorn, Jr.

Lothrop, Lee & Shepard Company

A Division of William Morrow & Company, Inc., N.Y.

Books by Hannah Lyons Johnson
with photographs by Daniel Dorn, Jr.

Picture the Past: 1900-1915
Let's Make Jam
From Seed to Jack-O'-Lantern
Let's Bake Bread
Let's Make Soup

illustrated by Tony Chen

Hello, Small Sparrow

Photo on page 31 by Ray R. Kriner (Cook College)

3   4   5   6   7   8   9   10

Library of Congress Cataloging in Publication Data

Johnson, Hannah Lyons.
    From apple seed to applesauce.

    SUMMARY: An introduction to the life cycle of the apple from seed to harvest. Includes a recipe for homemade applesauce

    1. Apple—Juvenile literature. [1. Apple]
I. Dorn, Daniel. II. Title.
SB363.J63   634′.11   76-52944
ISBN 0-688-41790-6   ISBN 0-688-51790-0 lib. bdg.

For my good and special friends—
Dan, Judy, Cassie and Nancy Dorn

My thanks to Daniel Dorn, Sr.; Mr. E. G. Christ, Extension Pomologist at Rutgers University; and especially to Mr. William E. Smith, Part Owner and Farm and Orchard Production Manager of Delicious Orchards, Colts Neck, New Jersey, for the many hours he so willingly gave.

A is for apples . . . red, yellow or green, hard or soft, sweet or tart. Apples are beautiful to look at, wonderful to smell and scrumptious to eat baked in a pie, simmered into sauce or just as they come from the trees. Apples in some form can be eaten the whole year through. Apple juice, apple salad, apple dumplings, pork chops baked with apples, and apple cake are just a few of the ways that apples can be prepared.

For centuries, apples have been a favorite fruit of people from many lands. They were especially important to the early American settlers from Europe. These people planted apple orchards with seeds and seedling trees brought from their homelands. Apples were one of the few fresh fruits that could be stored for use through the winter and spring in those days before refrigeration. They were kept cool underground in root cellars or specially dug pits. Cider made from apples was one of the favorite drinks of the settlers.

As Americans moved westward, a man named John Chapman (born in 1774) joined the pioneer people. For forty years, John wandered throughout the Ohio River Valley carrying the Bible and a cloth sack filled with apple seeds. He planted orchards wherever he stopped, and gave apple seeds and seedling trees to anyone who wanted them. People nicknamed him "Johnny Appleseed."

Apple growing today is much more scientific and complicated than it was in the days of Johnny Appleseed. Very few apple trees are grown from seed anymore. Trees grown from seed are called *chance seedlings*. There is no way to be sure just what variety of apple will grow on chance seedling trees.

There are many apple varieties grown in America today. The five most popular are: Red Delicious, Golden Delicious, Rome Beauty, McIntosh and Jonathan. These apples were all discovered growing on trees that began as chance seedlings.

RED DELICIOUS

GOLDEN DELICIOUS

ROME BEAUTY

McINTOSH

JONATHAN

5

Apple trees can be grown anywhere in the world where the weather is right. Summers must be sunny with at least 100 days without frost. There must also be enough rain. Winters must be cold enough for the apple trees to lose their leaves and rest. The winter temperature can be as warm as 45° above zero Farenheit and as cold as 30° below zero Farenheit.

In the warm days and cool nights of late summer and early autumn, apples are heavy and ripe for picking. But the apple grower works all year round so that the apples will be ripe and ready to harvest.

The job begins sometime in January or February when the bare apple trees are resting or *dormant*. This is when the trees in the orchard are trimmed or *pruned*. Old, dead and diseased branches are cut off, which encourages the growth of new, healthy branches. The apple trees are

pruned into a triangle or pyramid shape, so the upper branches won't shade the lower ones. This is important because all of the leaves use sunlight, air and water to make food for the rest of the tree. Very sharp saws on the ends of long poles are used for high pruning. Low pruning is done with sharp handsaws or clippers.

By late March or early April, the weather is usually warmer and the soil has dried out from the winter rain and snow. Often, small new trees are planted at this time to replace old ones or to add new varieties to the orchard. The apple farmer buys these young trees from a nursery so he can be certain they will grow the kind of apple he wants. These trees have not been grown from seed, but are grown by means of *grafting* and *budding*.

Grafting and budding are done on small one-year-old trees. A one-year-old tree is nothing more than a slender whip with roots beneath it.

To graft, a young twig, called a *scion*, is cut from the variety of apple tree to be formed. The scion contains a bud from which twigs and leaves will grow. This scion is inserted into a slit made on the top of the whip (1, 2). The two parts are bound together, until the scion and whip grow together, creating a new young tree (3, 4). This process is called *whip grafting*.

1

2

3

13

Budding is done by peeling a small section containing a bud from the green bark of a young twig (1). This bud section is slipped into the whip of a one-year-old tree where the green bark has been split and peeled back (2, 3). The bud section will grow onto the whip, forming a new tree (4). This tree will someday produce the same variety of apple that grew on the tree from which the bud was taken.

Budding and grafting are the only ways to grow trees that will bear exactly the variety of apple wanted. These methods can also be used on older, larger trees to change the variety.

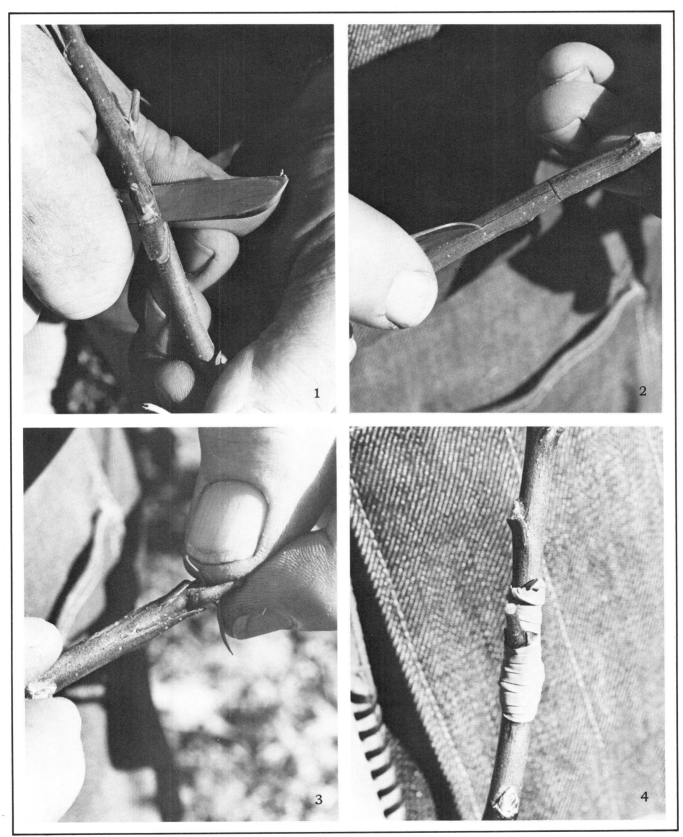

15

Some apple farmers plant their new trees in the spring, while other farmers plant them in the fall. In southern orchards, new trees can be planted even during the winter.

New trees are given *fertilizer* every year for two to three years, until they bear apples. Then they are fertilized only when they show signs, such as yellow leaves and poor apple growth, that fertilizer is needed. Fertilizer helps the trees grow strong and healthy.

Many new apple trees planted today are of the *dwarf* type. They generally do not grow as high or as large as standard-sized trees. But they produce a great amount of fruit for their size. Since their root systems are shallow, they often need extra support, such as fences or trellises, to keep them from blowing over in storms and strong winds.

As the spring days grow warmer and longer, the trees in the apple orchard begin to green up. Buds on the dark branches slowly develop into leaves.

When the leaves are about one-sixteenth of an inch long, the apple farmer begins spraying with *fungicides*. Fungicides help control diseases, such as apple scab and powdery mildew, which attack apple trees. Apple scab disease causes black spots to form on the undersides of the leaves. If it is controlled, there will be no scab spots later on the fruit. Powdery mildew disease makes the leaves look as if they have been sprinkled with white powder, and destroys the new growth. Fungicide spraying continues every two weeks until bloom time. Rain washes fungicides off the leaves, so after a rain the tree must be sprayed again.

Chemicals that kill insects, called *pesticides,* are also used. An oil pesticide is sprayed on the trees when the leaf buds first open. This spraying is sometimes done from a helicopter. The oil kills any spider mite eggs that might be on the trees. If the spider mites are allowed to hatch, their feeding makes yellow specks on the leaves and also causes the apples to be small and misshapen.

21

Bloom time is perhaps the most important and certainly the most beautiful time in the orchard. The apple trees will bloom anytime between late March or early June, depending on the weather and where the orchard is located. Trees in southern orchards bloom earlier than those in northern orchards. Apple blossoms can be deep pink, light pink or white, and grow in clusters of five. The center bloom, usually the largest and the first to bloom, is called the king flower. Each apple blossom has five petals and contains both male and female parts.

23

The male part is called the *stamen*. It has two sections. There is a long slender stem called the *filament*. On top of the filament is a small knob called the *anther*. There are twenty stamens sticking out from the center of each flower. They are very easy to see.

ANTHER

FILAMENT

25

The female part of the blossom is called the *pistil*. The pistil is a long slender tube which divides at the top into five smaller tubes called *styles*. Each style is topped by a round sticky knob called a *stigma*.

At the base of the pistil, under the flower petals, is a small bulb called the *ovary*. Inside the ovary are five seed cavities called *carpels*. Each carpel contains two tiny *ovules*. These female ovules will grow into apple seeds when they are joined with the male pollen.

ANTHER

FILAMENT

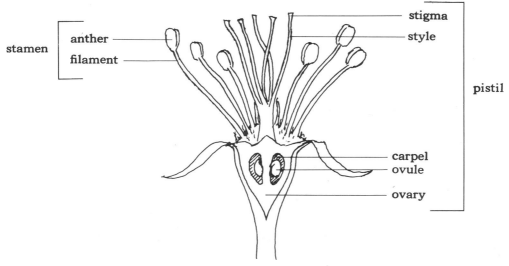

stamen

anther

filament

stigma

style

pistil

carpel

ovule

ovary

Although apple flowers have both male and female parts, most apple trees need pollen from another kind of apple tree to produce fruit. That is why there are almost always several varieties of apple trees in one orchard.

The apple farmer depends a lot on his machines, workers and tools, but when the trees are in bloom he needs the help of a friend in nature—the honey bee. If it were not for the honey bee, there would be few apples.

When about twenty-five percent of the trees are in bloom, boxes of bees are brought into the orchard by bee-keepers. The boxes are placed throughout the rows of trees.

The honey bee is attracted to the apple flowers by their sweet nectar and sticky pollen, which it collects to make honey and wax. While the bee is in the apple flower, tiny grains of pollen are knocked off the anthers onto its fuzzy body. The grains of pollen stick to the bee's body as it travels from flower to flower and tree to tree. When the bee visits another flower, a tiny pollen grain may be knocked off and fall onto the sticky stigma. This is called *pollination*. The pollen grain grows down through the tube of the style. When it reaches a carpel below, it joins with an ovule. This is called *fertilization*. When all or most of the ovules are fertilized, they will grow into apple seeds. At the same time, the walls of the ovary grow thicker and thicker, becoming the flesh of the apple. Without pollination and fertilization, the tiny apples would not develop.

ANTHER

FILAMENT

After fertilization takes place, the blossom petals start to fall and the beekeepers take their boxes of tiny pollinators away from the orchard. Now the apple farmer begins spraying again and continues into the summer. Fungicides are used to protect the apples from rot diseases. Pesticides are used to kill any insects that might attack the tree and its small, growing fruit. The apple farmer didn't dare spray during blossom time because the pesticides would have killed the bees. Aphids, apple maggots and codling moths are only a few of the many insects that can ruin an apple crop by eating the leaves or the fruit or both. Spraying of pesticides on the late-ripening varieties continues until the first part of August. Pesticide spraying is stopped sooner on varieties that ripen early. Fungicides are used up to two weeks before the apples are picked.

33

Sometimes after petal fall, there are too many little apples crowded together on the branches. Some of these apples fall off naturally to make room for the others to grow well. The apple farmer might also spray the trees with a chemical to make the unwanted apples drop.

If there are dry spells during the summer, the trees are watered. Sometimes irrigation pipes are placed in the orchard row so that water can be pumped from brooks, ponds, or wells to the thirsty trees.

During the summer, the apples grow larger and larger until they are finally ripe. The best way to tell if they are ripe enough for picking is simply to taste one. The farmer also tests for ripeness by measuring the sugar content of the apples with a special device called a *refractometer*. Different apple varieties ripen at different times. Some, like Rhode Island Greening and Twenty-Ounce Pippin, are ready in midsummer. McIntosh are usually ready in late summer, while Red Delicious are ripe in early fall. Golden Delicious and Staymen Winesap are picked in mid-fall.

Apples to be sold as fresh fruit are carefully picked by hand. Each picker wears a bag over his shoulder which he loads with apples. Full bags are emptied into big bins, which, when filled, are sent to a storage and packing plant. (If the apples are to be used to make foods, such as applesauce or cider, they are sometimes removed from the trees by mechanical shakers.) Some apple farmers store, pack and sell their crops at their own orchards. Others sell their apples to people who take care of storage, packing and marketing for them.

37

Since apples cannot be harvested year-round, they are stored so that people can buy them throughout the year. Apples to be stored for a long time are picked when they are less ripe than those to be stored for a shorter time. Even after an apple is picked, it continues to ripen until it finally overripens and then rots. The rotting process is nature's way of releasing the seeds from the fruit. The seeds are meant to grow into new trees.

Fresh-picked apples are washed, dried and sorted before they are marketed or put into cold storage. Since apples usually freeze at about 29° above zero Farenheit, most varieties are stored at about 31° above zero Farenheit. In some types of cold storage, the oxygen content of the air is also lowered. This, along with the cold temperature, slows down the natural ripening process of the apples and keeps them fresh. Even at home, apples should be stored in the refrigerator to keep them at their best.

One of the nicest and easiest ways to enjoy apples is to make them into sauce. Ask an adult to help you with this recipe because you will be using a sharp knife and cooking on a hot stove.

Homemade Applesauce

Ingredients
6 large, tart apples, such as McIntosh
½ cup water
½ cup sugar

1. Scrub the apples with a vegetable brush to remove any insecticides or fungicides. Cut them into quarters.
2. Put the apples and ½ cup water into a heavy pot. Put the pot on the stove and turn the burner to high until the water starts to boil.
3. Turn the burner to low. Cover the pot and simmer for 20 minutes. Stir the apples every few minutes with a wooden spoon to keep them from sticking to the bottom of the pot. Some apples are drier than others, so you may have to add more water.
4. Using pot holders, remove the pot from the stove and let the cooked apples cool for about 20 minutes.
5. Place a large strainer or colander over a nice big mixing bowl and pour the apples and the cooking water into the strainer or colander. Using a wooden spoon, press the

apples through the holes of the strainer or colander. The apple skins and pits will be left to throw away.

6. Add ½ cup sugar to the warm, strained apples and mix well. Some apples are sweeter than others, so you might like to use more or less sugar. Brown sugar or honey can also be used. Sprinkle in a little cinnamon if you like.

Your applesauce can be eaten warm or you can chill it in the refrigerator first. It can also be frozen. This recipe makes about 2 cups of applesauce. It can easily be doubled if you want to make more sauce.

The next time you crunch into an apple and the fragrant juice runs down your chin, remember, it took a year of hard work to produce it. Man and nature worked together to develop a perfect fruit for you to enjoy.